D0880764

AWESOME DOGS

# Golden Retrievers

by Chris Bowman

BLASTOFF!
2
READERS

BELLWETHER MEDIA • MINNEAPOLIS, MN

Note to Librarians, Teachers, and Parents:

**Blastoff! Readers** are carefully developed by literacy experts and combine standards-based content with developmentally appropriate text.

**Level 1** provides the most support through repetition of high-frequency words, light text, predictable sentence patterns, and strong visual support.

**Level 2** offers early readers a bit more challenge through varied simple sentences, increased text load, and less repetition of high-frequency words.

**Level 3** advances early-fluent readers toward fluency through increased text and concept load, less reliance on visuals, longer sentences, and more literary language.

**Level 4** builds reading stamina by providing more text per page, increased use of punctuation, greater variation in sentence patterns, and increasingly challenging vocabulary.

**Level 5** encourages children to move from "learning to read" to "reading to learn" by providing even more text, varied writing styles, and less familiar topics.

Whichever book is right for your reader, Blastoff! Readers are the perfect books to build confidence and encourage a love of reading that will last a lifetime!

This edition first published in 2016 by Bellwether Media, Inc.

No part of this publication may be reproduced in whole or in part without written permission of the publisher. For information regarding permission, write to Bellwether Media, Inc., Attention: Permissions Department, 5357 Penn Avenue South, Minneapolis, MN 55419.

Library of Congress Cataloging-in-Publication Data

Bowman, Chris, 1990- author.
  Golden Retrievers / by Chris Bowman.
     pages cm. – (Blastoff! Readers. Awesome Dogs)
  Summary: "Relevant images match informative text in this introduction to golden retrievers. Intended for students in kindergarten through third grade"– Provided by publisher.
  Audience: Ages 5-8
  Audience: K to grade 3
  Includes bibliographical references and index.
  ISBN 978-1-62617-241-8 (hardcover: alk. paper)
  1.  Golden retriever–Juvenile literature. 2.  Hunting dogs–Juvenile literature.  I. Title.
  SF429.G63B69 2016
  636.752'7–dc23
                          2015008702

Text copyright © 2016 by Bellwether Media, Inc. BLASTOFF! READERS and associated logos are trademarks and/or registered trademarks of Bellwether Media, Inc. SCHOLASTIC, CHILDREN'S PRESS, and associated logos are trademarks and/or registered trademarks of Scholastic Inc.

Printed in the United States of America, North Mankato, MN.

# Table of Contents

# What Are Golden Retrievers?

Golden retrievers are smart and sweet dogs.

They are known for their **loyalty** and playfulness. This makes them a favorite **breed** for families.

Golden retrievers have long, straight noses.

Dark brown eyes and floppy ears give them a friendly look.

Golden retrievers have big bodies. Their outer fur is soft. It can be wavy or straight.

They also have thick **undercoats** to keep them warm.

This breed has a golden **coat**.

Some of the dogs have dark golden fur. Others are lighter in color.

Lord
Tweedmouth

In the 1800s, Lord Tweedmouth of Scotland was looking for a good bird-hunting dog.

He also wanted a loyal and happy pet.

Scotland

N
W E
S

Lord Tweedmouth liked yellow dogs. He bought a golden puppy from a litter of black retrievers.

He **bred** it with another type
of hunting dog.

He used the golden puppies to continue his new breed.

## Golden Retriever Profile

long nose

floppy ears —

— golden fur

Life Span: 10 to 12 years

Trainability:

1   2   3   4   5   6

Hardest to train          Easiest to train

Today, the **American Kennel Club** places golden retrievers in its **Sporting Group**.

Golden retrievers are **athletic** dogs. They enjoy playing outside.

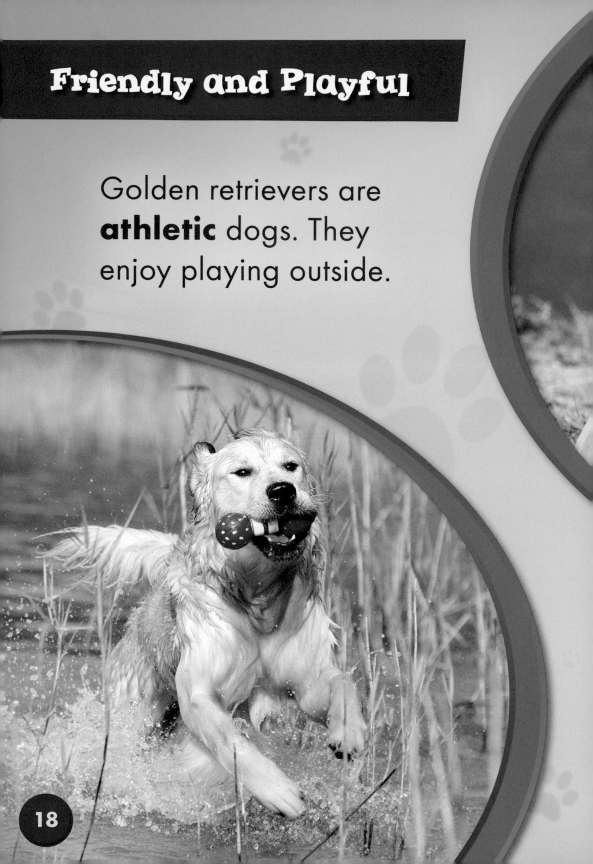

They are also quick learners.
Families and hunters like their
energy and **intelligence**.

Their need to please makes them good **service dogs**.

Some golden retrievers even work for the police or military. They love having a job to do!

# Glossary

**American Kennel Club**—an organization that keeps track of dog breeds in the United States

**athletic**—being strong, fit, and active

**bred**—purposely mated two dogs to make puppies with certain qualities

**breed**—a type of dog

**coat**—the hair or fur covering an animal

**intelligence**—the ability to learn and be trained

**loyalty**—having constant support for someone

**service dogs**—dogs trained to help people who have special needs perform daily tasks

**Sporting Group**—a group of dog breeds that are active and need regular exercise

**undercoats**—layers of short, soft hair or fur some dog breeds have to keep warm

# To Learn More

## AT THE LIBRARY

Barnes, Nico. *Golden Retrievers*. Minneapolis, Minn.: Abdo Kids, 2015.

Bodden, Valerie. *Retrievers*. Mankato, Minn.: Creative Education, 2014.

Landau, Elaine. *Golden Retrievers Are the Best!* Minneapolis, Minn.: Lerner Publications Co., 2010.

## ON THE WEB

Learning more about golden retrievers is as easy as 1, 2, 3.

1. Go to www.factsurfer.com.

2. Enter "golden retrievers" into the search box.

3. Click the "Surf" button and you will see a list of related web sites.

With factsurfer.com, finding more information is just a click away.

# Index

The images in this book are reproduced through the courtesy of: Irina Danilova, front cover; Margarita Borodina, p. 4; Martin Valigursky, p. 5; In Green, p. 6; Northsweden, p. 7; Mikkel Bigandt, p. 8; Robert Pickett/ Alamy, p. 9; Juniors Bildarchiv/ SuperStock/ Age Fotostock, pp. 10, 15; Eric Isselee, p. 11 (left); Andresr, p. 11 (right); Bain News Service/ Library of Congress, p. 12; cynoclub, p. 13; Zuzule, p. 14; Rita Kochmarjova, p. 16; Blinka, p. 17; AnetaPics, p. 18; HTeam, p. 19; Monkey Business Images, p. 20; Björn Nordien/ Alamy, p. 21.